OnBoard
ACADEMICS

I0220716

Language Fun

© 2015 OnBoard Academics, Inc
Portsmouth, NH
800-596-3175
www.onboardacademics.com
ISBN: 978-1-63096-041-4

OnBoard Academic's books are specifically designed to be used as printed workbooks or as on-screen instruction. Each page offers focused exercises and students quickly master topics with enough proficiency to move on to the next level.

OnBoard Academic's lessons are used in over 25,000 classrooms to rave reviews. Our lessons are aligned to the most recent governmental standards and are updated from time to time as standards change. Correlation documents are located on our website. Our lessons are created, edited and evaluated by educators to ensure top quality and real life success.

Interactive lessons for digital whiteboards, mobile devices, and PCs are available at www.onboardacademics.com. These interactive lessons make great additions to our books.

You can always reach us at customerservice@onboardacademics.com.

Fun with Puns

Key Vocabulary

pun

play on words

homonym

Pun

What happened when the red ship and the blue ship collided?

All of the survivors were marooned!

This is an example of **a pun**: a play on words involving two words which sound the same or similar, but which have different meanings.

maroon	*adjective*	dark red formed with blue and red
marooned	*noun*	stranded on an island after a shipwreck

Puns

Use the suggestions to complete these puns.

South of Peru, the weather can be [   ].

Please lower your voice. Shouting isn't [   ].

The car stopped because it wanted a [   ].

I was ill for a while, but the time just [   ] by.

There are cows over there? Yes, I [   ].

| flu | break | Chile | herd | aloud |

Write the homonym below each of the words.

| flu | break | Chile | herd | aloud |

Complete the puns.

It wasn't a fancy aircraft, it was quite [   ] .

Lots of plants grow alongside [   ] 54.

Big discounts during the boat yard [   ] !

If the teacher sees them, he'll [   ] them.

My lazy hero is my [   ] .

———————————————

Can you write a punning sentence using these words?

lends	lens	_____ _____
morning	mourning	_____ _____
pain	pane	_____ _____
rap	wrap	_____ _____
senses	census	_____ _____

Complete the sentences to create a pun and write the homonym under the blank line.

The stitches at the end of my pants didn't _____
that straight.

I said to the bus driver that the cost hike wasn't that _____.

My Grampa was _____ for driving without his glasses.

Those chickens smell really _____.

They said they would rent it to us for the _____
amount of money.

fare   cited   leased   fowl   seam
foul   fair   sighted   least   seem

Imagery

Key Vocabulary

imagery

poetry

www.onboardacademics.com

Strong Images

> A **poem** is a composition written to convey experiences, ideas, or emotions in a **vivid and imaginative way**.

Which poem creates a stronger image?

We were hiking
When it got wet
And windy outside.
So we found a cave
And stood inside
Sheltering from the rain.

Sheltering in a Cave by Owen

Sheltering in a Cave by Owen

We sheltered in its yawning mouth
As the wind began to wail
And whip-like cracks from high above
Drove us from the trail.
But the jagged light that lit this space
Illuminated every frightened face.
"Are we alone in this place?"

Imagery

Imagery uses descriptive language that appeals to the five senses to help create an emotional response in the reader.

Sheltering in a Cave by Owen

We sheltered in its yawning mouth
As the wind began to wail
And whip-like cracks from high above
Drove us from the trail.
But the jagged light that lit this space
Illuminated every frightened face.
"Are we alone in this place?"

Imagery Appeals to Our Five Senses

Highlight imagery in each sentence and then write the which sense it appeals to next to the sentence.

I hear my boots slosh through the puddles

As the cold rain splatters against my face.

I wipe the taste of moldy bark from my lips

And inhale the musty stench of dirt

As I watch the leaves tumble across the sky.

Using words or phrases that describe sight, sound, taste, smell or touch can help create mental images for the reader.

Words and Senses

Sort the words by the sense to which they appeal.

sight	sound	taste	smell	touch

acrid   silky   knobby   salty   syrupy

twitter   foul   gnarled   boom   murky

_____

Identify the sense being used in each line of the poem.

	The fiery glow of autumn
	Brings the aroma of roasting pumpkin seeds.
	The children dance amid the rustle of leaves
	Until the day grows dim.
	They skip home, snug in their layers of wool,
	Heading toward the sweetness of simmering cider.

touch	taste	sound	smell	sight

Strong Words

Choose a word that conveys a stronger emotion.

Strong words can help make
the imagery more vivid.

skinny	razor-thin
wet	
bright	
smooth	
windy	
warm	
short	

blustery

stumpy

slimy

silky

dazzling

cozy

Strong Imagery

From the sentences below, create phrases with stronger imagery.

The dog **walked** along the path.

The kids kept **shouting out** new ideas.

A bird **sang on the** branch.

The thunder **boomed** overhead.

Name_____

Imagery Quiz

1. Imagery uses vivid language to help capture a reader's imagination. True or false?

2. Which word best creates imagery of sunlight?
    a. covering
    b. radiating
    c. shining
    d. spreading

3. Choose the sentence with the most imagery.
    a. The kitten ferociously batted at the ragged toy.
    b. The cat sat in the corner.
    c. The dog barked at the neighbor.
    d. The bird chirped loudly.

4. Which sentence uses sound to create imagery?
    a. The tree branches swayed in the wind.
    b. Scents of wood burning wafted through the air
    c. The chill of the breeze made my nose turn red.
    d. The wind whispered like a child.

5. Which sense is used to create imagery in the following sentence: Their uniforms were satiny smooth agains their skin. _____

Fun with Puns Quiz

We don't want to ruin the fun with puns so no quiz. Just make up some fun puns to use on your friends.

Figurative Language

Key Vocabulary

figurative language

hyperbole

personification

metaphor

alliteration

simile

onomatopoeia

Figurative Language

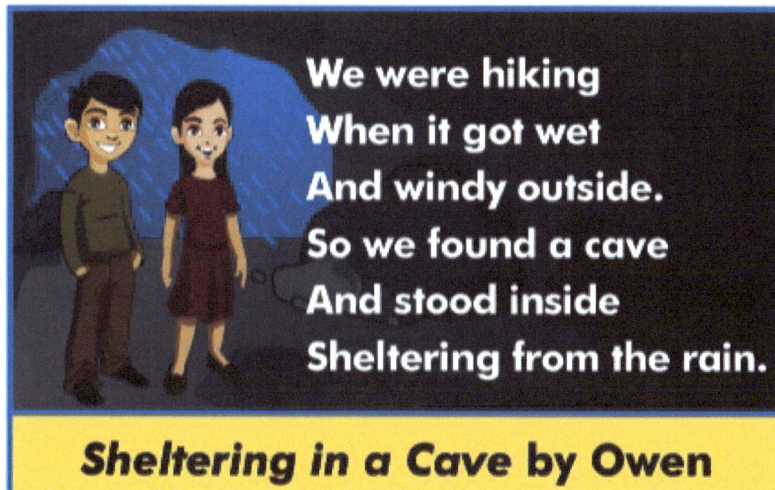

We were hiking
When it got wet
And windy outside.
So we found a cave
And stood inside
Sheltering from the rain.

Sheltering in a Cave by Owen

Figurative language makes writing more vivid and interesting, and helps to create powerful mental images and to invoke emotional responses.

_____

Now read the poem with figurative language added.

We sheltered in its yawning mouth as the wind began to wail and whip-like cracks from high above drove us from the trail. But, the jagged light that lit this space illuminated every frightened face. Are we alone in this place?

The Senses

> Figurative language that uses the five senses to create strong mental images is called imagery.

Label each passage with the sense that it invokes.

	The raw chicken breast was wet and slippery, and seemed to be trying to wriggle free.
	The grapefruit had an intense zing.
	The balloon sailed high into the puffy cotton candy clouds.
	The foul stench of the rotting corpse hung on the room like a heavy curtain.
	"Stand still, sonny!" hissed the old lady as she stood among her bad-tempered geese.

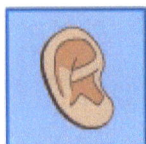

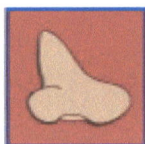

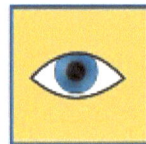

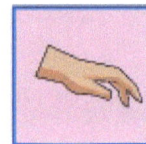

Similes and Metaphors

> A **simile** compares two unlike things using as or like; one thing is said to be *like* another. In a **metaphor**, one thing is said to be another. Metaphors also include figures of speech that help to vividly describe something in a non-literal or idiomatic way. For example, "My uncle is rolling in dough." *Dough* is a metaphor for money, and *rolling in it* is a metaphor for having lots of something.

———————————

Underline the similes and metaphors in this passage.

It's as plain as day that we need to reduce our use of carbons. One great way to do this would be to harness the power of the sun. I thought this would be a piece of cake, but my dad said that it's actually as difficult as a Greek puzzle to capture and store solar energy efficiently. That took the wind out of my sails a little. But it did give me another bright idea. Wind is a great clean energy source, and since we live in Chicago, it really should be as simple as ABC to find all of the wind we need.

Poems

Poems are usually extended metaphors.

> **They seem to be about one thing, in this case, making a choice about which direction to go in a wood, but are a metaphor for something else.**
>
> **What is the metaphor in this poem?**

The Road Not Taken − Robert Frost

Two roads diverged in a yellow wood,
And sorry I could not travel both
And be one traveler, long I stood
And looked down one as far as I could
To where it bent in the undergrowth;

Then took the other, as just as fair
And having perhaps the better claim,
Because it was grassy and wanted wear;
Though as for that, the passing there
Had worn them really about the same,

And both that morning equally lay
In leaves no step had trodden black
Oh, I kept the first for another day!
Yet knowing how way leads on to way,
I doubted if I should ever come back.

I shall be telling this with a sigh
Somewhere ages and ages hence:
Two roads diverged in a wood, and I,
I took the one less traveled by,
And that has made all the difference.

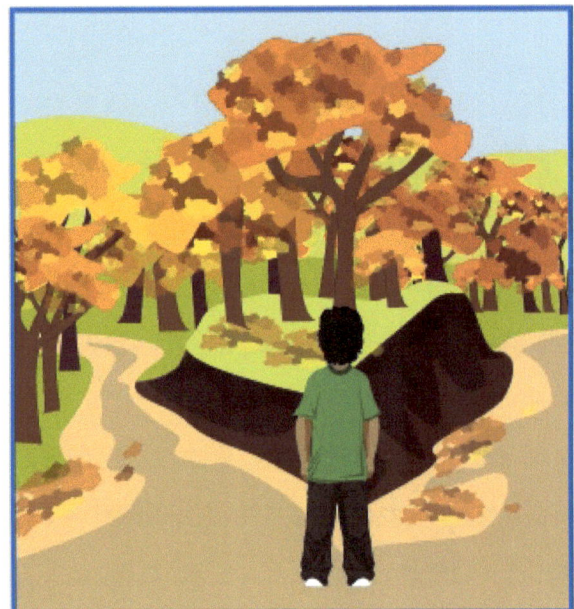

What is this poem about?

_____

_____

Alliteration

Alliteration is a figure of speech. A sound from either a vowel or a consonant is repeated to create a poetic effect.

_____

Use alliteration to tell the story of Little Red Riding Hood.

Girl with [_____] goes to [_____] .

Waylaid by [_____] on way through [_____] .

Cunning [_____] [_____] through [_____] .

[_____] on specs and [_____] [_____] .

Crimson- [_____] kid [_____] be [_____] .

[_____] [_____] [_____] off [_____] .

Slips   cuts   grandma's   canine   conned   teen

senior   clad   can't   goodies   simulates   wolf

teeth   woods   Titanic   tip   copse

Hyperbole is deliberate exaggeration used for emphasis or effect:
"I'm so hungry, I could eat a cow."
"You told me a thousand times already."

_____

Compete these sentences using hyperbole.

My Uncle Bert has got [ ] of money,

and his house is bigger than [ ] .

He's old as [ ] ,

and he repeats things a [ ] times,

but he's the best uncle [ ] .

Onomatopoeia

> **Onomatopoeia** is when the sound of a word suggests its meaning.

_____

Fill in the onomatopoeic word from the clue given.

①	someone at the door	
②	snake	
③	leaky faucet	
④	spasm of diaphragm	
⑤	angry lion	

Personification

> **Replace the highlighted word in each sentence to give the inanimate object a human trait or quality.**

Based on the instructions and the exercise what is personification?

Write the word above the yellow box.

The branches [**shook**] as the snow fell.

The [**old**] door would not open.

A wind [**blew**] in the night.

The old pick-up truck [**came**] to a halt.

The first rays of sunshine [**woke**] the boy.

| stubborn | ran | shivered | howled |
| groaned | blinded | greeted | crumpled |

_____

_____

_____

_____

The main elements of figurative language

Connect the colored box that represents part of the passage with its proper label.

■ **BRAZEN BANK BANDITS BAG BIG BUCKS** the headline in the *Eagle* ■ **screamed. Inspector McNulty was** ■ **as cunning as a fox, but he knew that this case would be** ■ **a tough nut to crack. Although he had** ■**a million other things to do, this case would be top priority. The** ■ **tick-tock of the old clock on the wall reminded him that he needed to tell his wife he was going to be late!**

☐ hyperbole ☐ personification ☐ alliteration

☐ metaphor ☐ simile   ☐ onomatopoeia

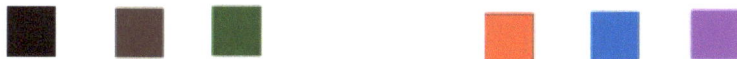

■ ■ ■   ■ ■ ■

Name_____

Figurative Language Quiz

1. The following sentence contains hyperbole:Everyone in the stadium was looking at me. True or false?

2. Which word is onomatopoeic?
   a. whisper
   b. float
   c. cut
   d. dense

3. Alliteration uses words that begin with the same letter. True or false?

4. Which sentence uses personification?
   a. The wind blew the leaves around.
   b. The leaves waved hello to the wind.
   c. The leaves rustled in the wind.
   d. The leaves made a soft sound in the wind.

5. What does the metaphor "Veiling their hurt with gentle smiles" mean?
   a. They are laughing hysterically.
   b. They were smiling although they were upset.
   c. They were smiling behind a garment.
   d. They were being mean-spirited.

      www.onboardacademics.com

Analogies

Key Vocabulary

analogy

synonym

antonym

homophone

Analogy

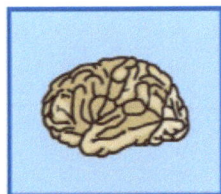

A [**brain**] is a lot like a [   ] .

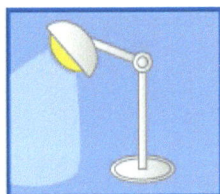

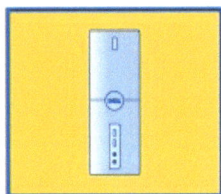

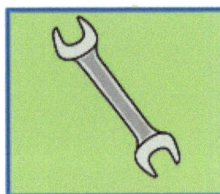

| lamp | computer | wrench |

You've just made an **analogy.** An analogy is a comparison of two or more objects suggesting that they are similar in some respects.

Synonym and Analogies

Find the synonym to complete the analogy.

KEY | **:** is to **::** as

shout : scream :: touch : feel

1 sad : miserable :: clean : [   ]

2 push : shove :: rough : [   ]

3 close : shut :: arrange : [   ]

4 look : search :: insist : [   ]

sort　　　**uneven**　　　**tidy**　　　**order**

Antonyms and Analogies

Find the antonym to complete the analogy.

fast : slow :: big : small

_____

1 rude : polite :: flexible : [ ]

2 catch : drop :: shout : [ ]

3 start : end :: past : [ ]

4 agree : argue :: noise : [ ]

whisper   future   rigid   silence

Relationships and Analogies

player **:** team **::** student **:** class   part **:** whole

hit **:** cry **::** tickle **:** laugh   cause **:** effect

_____

Consider the relationship and then complete the analogy.

1 hammer **:** tool **::** soccer **:** [   ]

2 boil **:** steam **::** freeze **:** [   ]

3 state **:** country **::** country **:** [   ]

4 sunrise **:** dawn **::** sunset **:** [   ]

Homophones and Analogies

Complete these homophone analogies and then create one of your own.

1 fare **:** fair **::** wait **:** ☐

2 blue **:** blew **::** course **:** ☐

3 their **:** there **::** air **:** ☐

4 ate **:** eight **::** side **:** ☐

5 to **:** too **::** ☐ **:** ☐

☐ **:** ☐ **::** ☐ **:** ☐

Name:

Analogies Quiz

1. An analogy is used to compare words. True or false?

2. Fabric is to dress as wood is to
    - a. tree
    - b. bench
    - c. cup
    - d. trumpet

3. Dog is to bark as lion is to
    - a. woof
    - b. roar
    - c. meow
    - d. sound

4. Snake is to bite as bee is to
    - a. yawn
    - b. buzz
    - c. jab
    - d. sting

5. Antarctica is to frigid as Africa is to
    - a. southern
    - b. continent
    - c. hot
    - d. Earth

Similes and Metaphors

Key Vocabulary

simile

metaphor

idiom

Similes and Metaphors

Simile

A simile is a figure of speech where two essentially unlike things are compared, typically using the words *like* or *as*.

"Nancy has a memory like an elephant."

Metaphor

A metaphor is a figure of speech that directly compares two essentially unlike things.

"I am an early bird, and my sister is a night owl."

In a simile, x is said to be like y;
in a metaphor, x is said to be y.

Label the statements from the passage.

Nancy remembered it was her aunt's birthday because she has a memory like an elephant, but she couldn't cycle to the mall to buy her aunt a gift because it was raining cats and dogs.

	Memory like an elephant.
	Raining cats and dogs.

Simile   **Metaphor**

Label Simile or metaphor

All the world's a stage.	
She's like the Bionic Woman.	
He turned as white as a ghost.	
Grammar is my Achilles' heel.	
It was as cold as ice.	

Label S for simile or M for metaphor.

1. We get along like a house on fire.

2. That test was easy. It was a piece of cake.

3. My dad won't budge. He's as stubborn as a mule.

4. Coach said she will cut me if I don't pull my socks up.

5. She is calm in a crisis. She is as cool as a cucumber.

Idioms

Idioms are frequently used in the business world. Can you guess this idiom?

Idioms are a bit like irregular metaphors. This means, that they are metaphors which, although widely understood, might be confusing to people who are new to the language or unfamiliar with the culture.

"I'm feeling under the weather."

"My dog kicked the bucket."

What do you think it means?

What do these other common business idioms mean?

| 1 | "Think outside of the box." |

| 2 | "Focus on the low-hanging fruit." |

| 3 | "We all need to be on the same page." |

Name_____

Similes and Metaphors Quiz

1. Metaphors compare things using the terms "like" or "as". True or false?

2. What does "that's music to my ears" mean?
    a. I can hear you clearly.
    b. That's exactly what I wanted to hear.
    c. I like music.
    d. Please turn up the sound a little.

3. Idioms are irregular metaphors. True or false?

4. Identify the simile that means "at high temperatures".
    a. Its a sauna in here.
    b. Its as hot as the equator
    c. We're sweating bullets
    d. I'm toasty

5. What does this metaphor mean? Con't cry over spilled milk.
    a. Clean up your mess.
    b. Buy more milk.
    c. Don't get upset over little mishaps.
    d. Drink orange juice instead of milk.

www.ingramcontent.com/pod-product-compliance
Lightning Source LLC
Chambersburg PA
CBHW042019080426

42735CB00002B/108